SCIENCE MISSIONS

Searching for Arctic Oil

Eve Hartman and Wendy Meshbesher

Chicago, Illinois

www.heinemannraintree.com
Visit our website to find out more information about Heinemann-Raintree books.

To order:
☎ Phone 888-454-2279
🖳 Visit www.heinemannraintree.com to browse our catalog and order online.

Edited by Adam Miller, Andrew Farrow, and Adrian Vigliano
Designed by Philippa Jenkins
Original illustrations © Capstone Global Library Ltd.
Illustrated by KJA-artists.com
Picture research by Tracy Cummins
Production by Alison Parsons
Originated by Dot Gradations
Printed and bound in China by South China Printing Company Ltd

14 13 12 11 10
10 9 8 7 6 5 4 3 2 1

Library of Congress Cataloging-in-Publication Data
Hartman, Eve.
  Searching for Arctic Oil / Eve Hartman and Wendy Meshbesher.
     p. cm. — (Science Missions)
  Includes bibliographical references and index.
  ISBN 978-1-4109-3822-0 (hc)
1. Petroleum—Juvenile literature.
2. Petroleum—Geology—Arctic regions—Juvenile literature.
3. Petroleum—Prospecting—Arctic Region—Juvenile literature. I. Meshbesher, Wendy.
II. Title.
  TN870.3.H37 2011
  622'.1828091632—dc22

2009053180

Acknowledgments
The author and publishers are grateful to the following for permission to reproduce copyright material: Age Fotostock ©idreamstock **p.10**; Age Fotostock ©Alaska Stock Images **p.12**; Alamy ©Danita Delimont **pp.34&35**; AP Photo/Mark Lennihan **p.36 bottom**; AP Photo **p.39**; Corbis ©Paul Souders **pp.4&5**; Corbis ©Peter Guttman **p.16**; Corbis ©Tim Thompson **p.18**; Corbis ©Steven Kazlowski/Science Faction **p.19**; Corbis ©Steven Kazlowski/Science Faction **p.21**; Corbis ©Bettmann **p.24**; Corbis ©Karen Kasmauski **p.26**; Corbis ©Grand Tour **p.27**; Corbis ©Steven Kazlowski/Science Faction **pp28&29**; Corbis ©Steven Kazlowski/Science Faction **p.41**; Corbis ©Paul Souders **pp.42&43**; Corbis ©Jon Hicks **p.44**; Getty Images/Johnny Johnson **p.7**; Getty Images/Chad Ehlers **pp.8&9**; Getty Images/Per Breiehagen **pp.14&15**; Getty Images **p.20**; Getty Images/Tony Waltham **pp.22&23**; Getty Images/ Andy Reynolds **p.31**; Getty Images **p.33**; Getty Images/Oli Scarff **p.36 top**; Getty Images/ Natalie B. Fobes **p.38**; Getty Images/Jean-Christian Bourcart **p.45**; Getty Images/Paul Edmondson **p.47**; Getty Images/John Warden **pp.48&49**; Photolibrary/Paul Lawrence **p.17**; Photolibrary/Steven Kazlowski **p.40**; Shutterstock/Armin Rose **pp.50&51**.

Cover photograph of an offshore oil platform reproduced with the permission of Getty Images/Ken Graham.

We would like to thank Daniel Block for his invaluable help in the preparation of this book.

Every effort has been made to contact copyright holders of any material reproduced in this book. Any omissions will be rectified in subsequent printings if notice is given to the publisher.

CONTENTS

Some words are printed in bold, **like this**. You can find out what they mean by looking in the glossary. You can also look out for them in the WORD STORE box at the bottom of each page.

O I L
I N   T H E
A R C T I C

The Arctic is one of the coldest, most remote places on Earth. Yet below it lies something of great value. That something is oil. Oil is also called **petroleum**. It is processed into fuels and is also used to make plastics.

Companies have been mining the world's oil for years. Many oil fields are now empty or close to empty. But other stores of oil, called reserves, have yet to be tapped. Scientists guess that about one-fourth of the world's remaining oil lies below the Arctic Ocean.

Mining oil from an ocean is not easy. It involves building platforms over the water. Below the platforms are shafts to the ocean floor that go deep into the ground beneath it. Then the oil must be shipped to the places where it is needed. Oil that is mined in the Arctic must be shipped a long way!

Should we expand oil drilling in the Arctic? Many people say yes. Others think that the risks are too high. As you read more about this debate, pay close attention to people's opinions and to the facts and evidence that they **cite** (refer to). This will help you form your opinion about drilling for Arctic oil.

The oil business

The United States, Canada, and Russia all border the Arctic Ocean. So does the island of Greenland, which is part of Denmark, as well as islands that are a part of Norway and Iceland. Oil is now being mined in lands claimed by all of these countries. The most significant mining has been in Prudhoe Bay, a region off the Alaskan coast that is part of the United States.

The Prudhoe Bay oil field is the largest oil field in North America. It was discovered in the 1960s by scientists working for two companies: the Atlantic Richfield Company, or ARCO (now a part of British Petroleum), and the Humble Oil Company (now part of Exxon Mobil). A few years later, with the approval of the U.S. government, these companies began work to tap the oil. Their efforts included the building of the **Alaska Pipeline**, which you will read about beginning on page 22.

Today, the mining at Prudhoe Bay is operated by three large, international oil companies: British Petroleum, Conoco-Phillips, and Exxon Mobil. As of 2009 these companies had produced 13 billion barrels of oil. That is a huge volume—about the same as the volume of water that flows over Niagara Falls in about six weeks! But while oil production continues today, it has a limited lifetime. Scientists estimate that the fields can efficiently produce only about 3 billion barrels more.

A new reserve

New oil wells are continuing to be developed in the Arctic. In 2009 the U.S. government granted Shell Oil the right to open new wells there. But the greatest reserves remain untapped by current U.S. law. These reserves are in the **Arctic National Wildlife Refuge (ANWR)**. Scientists estimate that ANWR oil fields hold between 6 and 16 billion barrels of oil.

People disagree about whether mining in ANWR would harm its native animals, such as these porcupine caribou.

Like other nature reserves and parks, the ANWR was established to protect the plants, animals, and people in the area. The animals include herds of caribou on land and whales in the water. Both of these animals are a source of food for the Inupiats, a group of Native Americans who live in the ANWR and along the Arctic coast.

Many people want the current laws kept in force. They argue that oil wells would be an ugly addition to a beautiful part of the world. They also argue that pollution from drilling would harm the animals and people that live there.

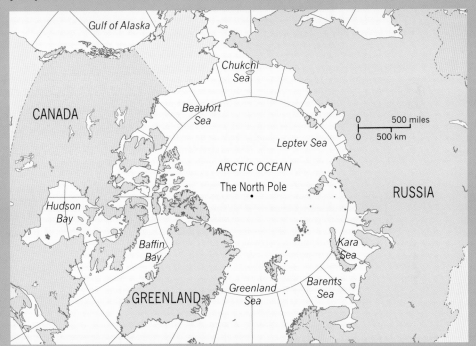

WORD STORE   **Arctic National Wildlife Refuge (ANWR)** region in Alaska set aside for wildlife, and a site of oil reserves along its coast

OIL:
AN INTRODUCTION

Does this scene look familiar? The photo on this page shows cars and highways in Los Angeles, California. But cities all across the world look much like this.

Beginning in the 1920s, the automobile became a very popular way to travel. Roads and highways were built for cars and trucks to drive on. People began using cars to drive to and from their homes, work, and shopping centers. People also fly on airplanes from city to city. These vehicles also ship a huge variety of goods—everything from abacuses to zucchinis—between places all over the world.

For this reason, modern life has come to depend on oil. Oil is a liquid used to make gasoline, which is the fuel that powers most cars. It is used to make diesel fuel, which powers trucks, as well as the fuel for airplanes. Oil is also used to make plastics.

Scientists have been studying ways to replace oil. Today, a few cars run on batteries, or on a combination of batteries and gasoline. In the future these cars may be improved and become more popular.

For the present, however, oil remains as important as ever. Without new supplies of oil, modern life would change very quickly.

The twisting hustle
and bustle of modern,
urban life: a freeway
interchange above Los
Angeles, California.

9

Ancient energy

Oil, along with coal and **natural gas**, are examples of **fossil fuels**. Fossils are the remains of ancient living things. When you use a fossil fuel, you are using the energy of a plant or animal that lived millions of years ago!

All of Earth's oil formed from the remains of algae or small animals that lived in ancient oceans. First, the living things died in the ocean, fell to the floor, and were buried. Then, very slowly, layers of rock built over the remains of these living things. The weight gradually squeezed them. They also were heated by Earth's interior.

Over time the remains slowly changed into different kinds of matter. Often they changed into a thick, black liquid, which is oil. They also changed into methane, which is natural gas. Natural gas often collects just above oil.

Beneath Earth's oceans, the process of making oil and natural gas has always been taking place. It is taking place right now! However, people have been using oil and other fossil fuels far faster than nature can replace them. And once a supply of fossil fuels is used for energy, it cannot be used again.

For this reason fossil fuels are described as nonrenewable resources. Once fossil fuels are gone, they are gone for good.

WORD STORE   **fossil fuel** fuel formed from remains of ancient organisms

OIL BELOW LAND?

HOW OIL FORMS

Oil is not always found below oceans. Oil is also found on land. These lands include the deserts of Saudi Arabia, mountainous lands in China, and the plains of eastern Texas and Oklahoma. But oil forms beneath oceans! So, why do we find oil below land? The reason is because Earth's continents and oceans slowly move across the planet. They also change size and shape. Places where oil is found now were under the ocean millions of years ago.

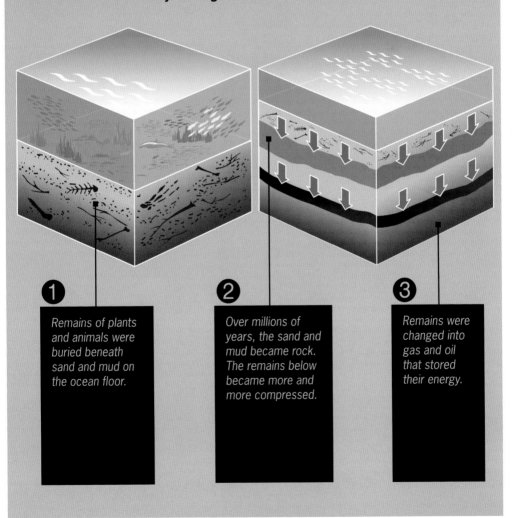

1 Remains of plants and animals were buried beneath sand and mud on the ocean floor.

2 Over millions of years, the sand and mud became rock. The remains below became more and more compressed.

3 Remains were changed into gas and oil that stored their energy.

These towers are part of an Alaskan oil refinery. In this photo you can clearly see the different levels of each tower. Check out page 13 to see how the towers work.

From rig to refinery

Oil is brought out of the ground by **oil rigs**, which are artificial islands built for mining oil from beneath the ocean floor. The oil they get is a thick, black liquid often called **crude oil**. It is a mixture of several different substances called **hydrocarbons**, plus small amounts of impurities. Hydrocarbons are compounds made only of the elements carbon and hydrogen.

All of the hydrocarbons in crude oil are useful, but not when they are mixed together. Scientists have found ways to **refine**, or separate, crude oil into its different parts. This is done at a place called an oil refinery.

Boiling oil

The illustration on page 13 shows how an oil refinery works. The crude oil is placed at the bottom of a tall tower. Then it is boiled. As the vapors rise up the tower, they condense back into liquids at different levels. Heavy hydrocarbons condense into liquids near the bottom of the tower. Lightweight hydrocarbons condense near the top.

After the hydrocarbons are separated, they are treated to make useful fuels. Oil companies make gasoline, diesel fuel, and jet fuel from mixtures of hydrocarbons and other compounds.

WORD STORE   **crude oil** oil that has not been refined
hydrocarbon compound made of carbon and hydrogen

Why are hydrocarbons such useful fuels? The reason is because of the chemical bonds inside them. The bond between a carbon and hydrogen atom contains a lot of energy. This bond easily breaks when the hydrocarbon is burned in oxygen. A lot of energy is released!

Engines that run on gasoline are called internal combustion engines. They combust, or burn, gasoline by combining it with oxygen at a high temperature. The energy that is released powers the engine.

Wood and plant products also contain bonds between carbon and hydrogen. These materials are also useful fuels. You use wood as a fuel when you burn it in a fireplace or at a campfire. Many people heat their homes or cook food with wood-burning stoves.

However, unlike hydrocarbons, wood contains significant amounts of oxygen and other elements. As a result wood would burn too slowly and release too little energy to be useful in an engine.

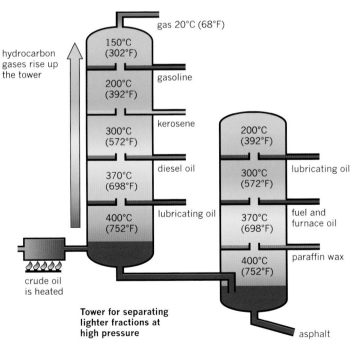

gas 20°C (68°F)

150°C (302°F)

hydrocarbon gases rise up the tower

200°C (392°F) gasoline

kerosene

300°C (572°F)

200°C (392°F)

370°C (698°F) diesel oil

300°C (572°F) lubricating oil

400°C (752°F) lubricating oil

370°C (698°F) fuel and furnace oil

400°C (752°F) paraffin wax

crude oil is heated

Tower for separating lighter fractions at high pressure

asphalt

Tower for separating heavier fractions at low pressure

During the refining process, the separated parts of crude oil hydrocarbons are called fractions. As the oil is boiled and becomes gas, the fractions rise to different levels depending on how small and light they are.

WORD STORE   **oil rig** artificial island built for mining oil
refine process of separating a substance into compounds

13

CHALLENGES OF THE
ARCTIC

Conditions in the Arctic present many difficult challenges for oil companies and their employees. Perhaps the biggest challenge is the weather.

In places across Earth, the Sun rises in the east every morning. It appears to climb in the sky, then slowly set to the west in the evening. The Sun climbs higher in the sky in summer than in winter. Summer days last longer, too.

The Sun also moves like this in the Arctic. But it never climbs very high in the sky. This is one reason why weather in the Arctic can be icy cold even during the summer. During the winter the Sun may appear for only a few hours every day, or not at all! Arctic winters are very dark and extremely cold.

Another challenge of working in the Arctic is the distance from cities and farms. Building and operating **oil rigs** requires a huge amount of equipment. Workers need beds, food, and fresh water. All of these things must be shipped to the work site, often from very far away.

Yet these challenges are only the beginning. The process of finding and drilling oil involves many complicated steps. Each step is necessary for success.

Gunning for oil

There is a lot of oil below the Arctic, but it is not everywhere. You can think of oil deposits as treasure chests that are buried beneath the ocean floor. To find these treasures, you could dig in random places and hope for the best. But that would take a very long time.

Instead of digging randomly, the **geologists** who work for oil companies begin their search by studying the ocean floor with sound. Sound waves travel through oil at a different speed than they travel through rocks and other materials.

As you might guess, very powerful sounds are needed for this type of study. To make these sounds, geologists and oil companies use giant air guns. The guns make loud, booming noises as they are dragged across the ocean floor. By measuring how these sounds travel, scientists can predict where oil deposits are.

This is a nuclear-powered Russian icebreaker ship. In this photo it is plowing through the ice of the Arctic Ocean, headed toward the North Pole.

WORD STORE   **exploratory rig** small oil rig built to search for oil deposits

Exploratory rigs like this one are often the next step after an air-gun search. If an exploratory rig is successful, larger rigs may follow.

Icebreakers and islands

In the Arctic much of the ocean is covered in ice, even in summer. So, ships called **icebreakers** are needed to drag the air guns. Icebreakers have very strong hulls that can break through a layer of ice on the ocean's surface. The hull is the outer wall of the ship.

After an air-gun search, oil companies usually build **exploratory rigs**. An exploratory rig is a small, relatively simple oil rig. Its purpose is for digging test wells into the ocean floor. If they produce oil, larger rigs will be built.

In warmer oceans, an exploratory rig is relatively easy to build. But the Arctic freezes over every winter. A rig cannot be built on the ice because the ice moves. So, oil companies often build islands out of gravel for the rig to rest on. When the rig's job is finished, the gravel island is dug up and moved to a new place.

No guarantees

Searching for oil is always risky! Exploring the floor of a warm ocean can cost millions of dollars. Exploring an icy ocean is even more expensive. There is no guarantee that a search will be successful.

WORD STORE   **geologist** scientist that studies Earth's surface and interior
icebreaker ship that can move through frozen water

Workers keep an oil platform operating at all times. Their job is not easy, especially in cold, Arctic weather.

Harsh conditions

If an exploratory rig has tapped oil, an oil company may then build an **oil platform**. An oil platform is a large oil rig. The platform holds the machinery needed to drill wells, and it is a temporary home to workers. Thirty or more wells might be drilled from the same platform into the ocean. Some wells are drilled straight down, while others are drilled at an angle.

In the Arctic, most oil platforms are totally enclosed to protect the workers inside. The platforms must be able to withstand thick ice and water temperatures that are near the freezing point of 0 °C (32 °F). The platforms must also be moved to new locations when wells run dry.

Moving the oil

After the oil is pumped, it must be stored or processed. In warmer oceans, pipelines are used to send the oil from platforms to the mainland. A pipeline is a network of pipes that carries oil across a long distance. But pipelines are often difficult to install in the Arctic. Instead the oil is usually stored in tanks. Then ships that can break through the ice carry the oil to shore. Trucks can carry the oil when the ice is thick enough.

Laws apply to each of these steps—exploring, drilling, and transportation. The purpose of many of these laws is to protect the environment from oil spills. Other laws protect the rights of workers. Some parts of the Arctic are claimed by different nations, as well as by native peoples. The laws and claims are not always clear.

WORD STORE **mammal** animal that makes milk for its young

Is drilling in the Arctic worth the expense and difficulty? The answer depends on the price of gasoline and other products made from oil. The answer also depends on risks to the environment, which you will learn more about as you read on.

NOISE POLLUTION

Drilling for oil can pollute the water when oil leaks or spills. But the search for oil can cause noise pollution, too.

The underwater air guns used to search for oil often create blasts that are louder than rocket launches. Search ships fire the guns as often as six times every minute, and for days or weeks in a row.

Evidence shows that these noises are harming ocean animals, especially whales. The noises damage the whales' hearing. Whales need to hear to communicate with one another and to find mates. Deaf whales may also become stranded on beaches.

"The federal government must stop pandering to [trying to please] the oil companies and start [protecting] these **mammals**," said David Dickson, the director of the Alaska Wilderness League. "We are asking them to follow the law."

Beluga whales live throughout the Arctic Ocean. Noise from air guns is harming their hearing.

WORD STORE   **oil platform** large oil rig, used after oil has been found

Living in Prudhoe Bay

About 50 people make their permanent home in Prudhoe Bay, Alaska, and communities near it. But at any given moment, thousands of workers live in the town and on the oil platforms. They stay there for a few weeks or months at a time. They spend the rest of their time elsewhere.

A dirt road leads south from Prudhoe Bay, and it is the only road in or out of town. The road leads to Fairbanks, Alaska, the nearest city, which is 800 kilometers (500 miles) away. The road is mostly used by trucks. Many people prefer to fly to and from Prudhoe Bay on airplanes or helicopters.

The winter climate is perhaps the biggest reason why few people want to live there. Climate is the yearly pattern of weather. From December to March, the temperature hardly ever rises above –18 °C (0 °F), and usually it is much colder. The Sun rises for shorter and shorter periods of time. From late November through January, it does not appear at all!

Workers live in apartments on the oil platforms. The apartments are small, but well furnished. They can be easily taken apart and put back together.

If you could choose where you wanted to work, would you choose Prudhoe Bay? Not many people would. This is why the workers are paid very well.

"It is extremely hard, dirty, dangerous, tiresome, and miserable work."

said one worker about his job in the Prudhoe Bay oil fields.

"That's why I'm not there anymore."

Arctic life

The town of Prudhoe Bay might disappear without the oil industry. But that is not the case for other towns and communities in northern Alaska.

Barrow, Alaska, lies even farther north than Prudhoe Bay. Barrow is the year-long home to a few thousand people. Most are Inupiats, a group of Native Americans. Many live by hunting whales, seals, fish, polar bears, and other Arctic animals. An airport provides the main way in and out of Barrow.

The border of the Arctic Ocean is dotted with small communities like Barrow. They are home to peoples who have lived there for many generations. Year after year, they meet the challenges of life in the Arctic. They want to keep meeting them, too.

Barrow, Alaska. This group of Inupiats is saying a prayer before a native crew leaves on a whaling trip.

THE
PIPELINE

After oil is mined from the Arctic, what happens to it next? Atlantic Richfield and other oil companies had to answer this question before they began drilling. Ordinary tanker ships could not reach the Arctic because of the ice. Using trucks or trains to carry the oil would be too costly.

The oil companies' solution was to build a pipeline. In 1975 construction began on a pipeline from Prudhoe Bay to the ocean port of Valdez, Alaska. Two years later the pipeline opened. Its official name is the Trans-Alaska Pipeline System, but it is often simply called the **Alaska Pipeline**.

At the time the Alaska Pipeline was the largest construction project of its kind. It remains very impressive, covering a distance of 1,300 kilometers (800 miles), over land which includes three mountain ranges, hundreds of rivers and streams, and several faults. A fault is a crack in Earth's crust where earthquakes often strike.

Oil companies spent $8 billion to build the pipeline. Today, more than 30 years after it was built, the pipeline has more than paid back that investment.

Building the pipeline

Building and running a pipeline is difficult in any location. But the environment of Alaska presents special challenges.

Oil must be kept at a high temperature—about 49 °C (120 °F)—to flow smoothly through a pipeline. This means the Alaska Pipeline must be very well insulated (protected from losing heat). Without the insulation, the cold weather would cool the oil very quickly.

In most places, pipelines are buried. But much of the Alaska Pipeline is on stilts. The reason is that the pipeline and the Alaskan tundra would damage each other. Tundra is ground that has a permanently frozen layer below the surface. The frozen layer is called permafrost. Even a little escaped heat from the pipeline could melt the tundra around it. The pressure of the frozen tundra could also crack the pipeline apart.

As the photo on page 23 shows, the Alaska Pipeline is not built in a straight line. Instead it crosses much of the countryside in a zigzag pattern. This helps the pipeline keep from cracking apart in an earthquake. The zigzag pattern is quite stable when the ground starts shaking.

The pipeline costs money to operate. Workers must staff pumping stations, inspect the pipeline, and make repairs to it. As of now the pipeline needs to carry 200,000 barrels a day to pay for itself. It now carries much more than this amount. But production from the Prudhoe Bay oil fields drops a little every year, as the oil fields are gradually emptied.

Experts guess that without a new source of oil, the pipeline will need to be closed by 2020. As discussed earlier, the most likely new source of oil is in the ANWR.

According to current law, the pipeline must be taken apart and removed when it is closed.

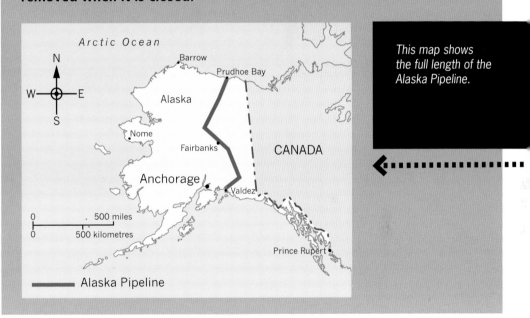

This map shows the full length of the Alaska Pipeline.

Not quite perfect

After more than 30 years in operation, the pipeline has proven itself very useful and safe. Only rarely has it been shut down. It has lasted through forest fires, earthquakes, and acts of vandalism (deliberate destruction). The pipeline is also inspected regularly and observed from airplanes.

Nevertheless, the pipeline system has spilled oil on occasion. The worst spill was in 2006, near Prudhoe Bay. It involved small pipes that fed into the main pipeline. The small pipes were rusty and burst apart. Thousands of gallons of oil were spilled.

End of the line

After its long journey across Alaska, oil finally arrives in the port of Valdez. Valdez is on the southern coast of Alaska. This location is ideal for shipping oil because it is free of ice all year long.

The port of Valdez, Alaska, is the southern end of the Alaska Pipeline. Tankers take over the job of carrying the oil.

In Valdez harbor, oil from the pipeline is stored in large tanks. Then the oil is transferred to tankers, which are ships that carry oil. The tankers bring the oil to refineries in California and elsewhere. Since the pipeline opened in 1977, more than 19,000 tankers have left Valdez filled with oil.

Unfortunately, in 1989 a tanker called the *Exxon Valdez* suffered a terrible accident. It spilled a huge amount of oil into the ocean waters south of Valdez. You will read more about this accident on page 39.

Since the accident many safety precautions have been put in place. All tankers are now escorted as they leave Valdez. They are also watched by the U.S. Coast Guard. Shipping companies are required to file plans to prevent spills, as well as plans to clean up any spills that may occur.

Shipping companies are also required to build new ships with two sets of hulls, one inside the other. Experts believe that if a ship strikes rocks or the shore, a double hull is more likely to hold oil than a single hull.

Russian scientist Dmitry Mendeleyev is famous for inventing the periodic table of the elements. But he also was the first person to propose that pipes be used to carry oil. He did so in 1863, when the oil industry was just beginning.

Today, pipelines are operated all over the world. Many carry oil from oil fields to shipping docks. Others carry **natural gas**, water, and even beverages.

The longest underwater pipeline is the Langeled Pipeline at 1,166 kilometers (725 miles). It brings natural gas from Norway to the United Kingdom. Nearly all of the pipeline is under the North Sea, the arm of the Atlantic Ocean that separates the two countries.

Pipelines are used around the world for many purposes. This oil pipeline runs through Tasmania, Australia.

DRILLING IN ANWR:
THE CASE FOR

"Oil and gas production [can] go hand in hand with responsible environmental stewardship (careful management)."

Lisa Murkowski, Republican U.S. senator from Alaska.

For over 30 years, oil companies have been drilling oil in Prudhoe Bay and nearby oil fields. These fields still produce oil, but not as much as before. They eventually will run dry.

To many people the next logical step is to drill in the nearby **ANWR**. Workers and equipment could be readily moved to the ANWR. The front end of the **Alaska Pipeline** could be extended to reach it. Yet, as we have seen, the ANWR was established to protect wildlife, including animals that live on land and in the ocean. Laws protect the ANWR from many human activities, including drilling for oil.

Can oil be drilled in the ANWR without damaging wildlife and the environment? Many people say that yes, it can. These people include many citizens of Alaska and their representatives in the U.S. government. They want to change the laws and let drilling begin as soon as possible. To argue their case, they **cite** the safety record in Prudhoe Bay and the high demand for gasoline and other fuels.

In this chapter, you will read about the case for drilling in the ANWR. The next chapter will present the case against drilling.

A bull caribou outside of the oil town of Deadhorse, Alaska. A major issue in the debate over drilling in ANWR centers on the possible effects drilling would have on caribou herds and movements.

A disappearing resource

As discussed earlier, people everywhere have come to rely on oil. Yet oil is a nonrenewable resource. After an oil field is tapped, it is only a matter of time before it will be empty. Because people mine and use oil every day, Earth's total supply of oil is always decreasing.

This bar graph shows how oil use and production has changed in the United States. The facts are similar for other economically developed nations.

Since 1980 the amount of oil produced in the United States has been gradually declining. The demand for oil, however, has kept rising. By 2005 Americans were using more oil than ever before. Most of it was oil imported (brought in) from other countries.

Bridging the gap

Many people cite the high demand for oil as the most important reason to drill in the ANWR. They argue that Americans will continue to need oil to run cars, trucks, and airplanes. Because other nations are increasing their demand for oil, the United States should tap all of the oil available within its borders.

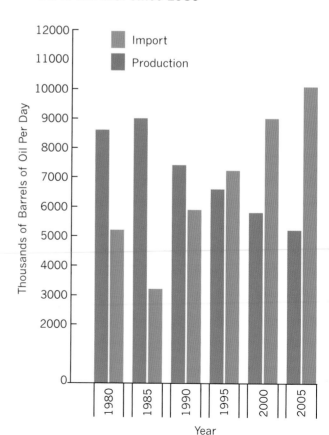

Oil in the U.S. since 1980

While oil use in the United States has risen sharply, the country's production of oil has dropped.

WORD STORE   **hydrogen fuel cell** battery-like device that runs on hydrogen and produces electricity

Several very large companies are in the oil and energy business. These companies include Exxon Mobil, Royal Dutch Shell, British Petroleum, Chevron, and Conoco-Phillips. Each of these companies operates all over the world.

Some people hope that oil from the ANWR will lower the price of gasoline, at least in the United States. However, many experts think this is unlikely. They argue that the ANWR would produce only a small amount of oil compared to the world's total supply. Because oil is sold globally, its price depends on global supply and demand.

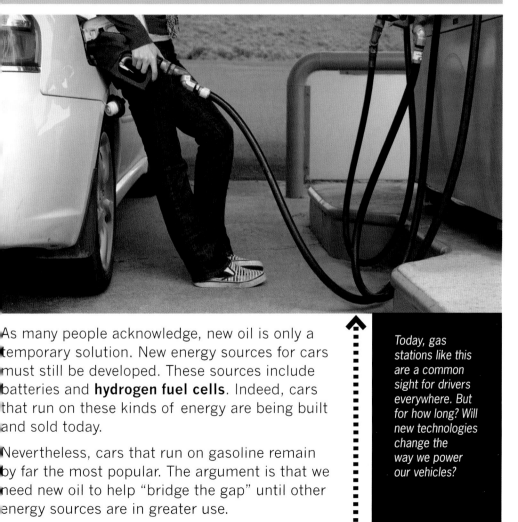

As many people acknowledge, new oil is only a temporary solution. New energy sources for cars must still be developed. These sources include batteries and **hydrogen fuel cells**. Indeed, cars that run on these kinds of energy are being built and sold today.

Nevertheless, cars that run on gasoline remain by far the most popular. The argument is that we need new oil to help "bridge the gap" until other energy sources are in greater use.

Today, gas stations like this are a common sight for drivers everywhere. But for how long? Will new technologies change the way we power our vehicles?

Environmentally friendly?

Many people who want to drill in the ANWR are also concerned about the environment there. But they claim that the oil industry would not do great harm to the animals of the Arctic or its native peoples. For evidence they cite the history of drilling in Prudhoe Bay.

Since drilling began in Prudhoe Bay, the populations of caribou, polar bears, and Arctic foxes have all increased or stayed about the same. No major oil spills have spoiled the bay, and the minor spills were cleaned up easily.

Oil companies also now use new, improved technology. The new wells are smaller and more efficient. If the wells on Prudhoe Bay were built today, they would take up about two-thirds of the amount of ocean space.

A new angle

In 2009 Alaska's representatives in the U.S. Congress proposed an interesting compromise. Their proposal would allow drilling in the ANWR, but only from its edges. **Oil platforms** would drill at an angle into the ocean floor off the ANWR coast. This is called **directional drilling**.

With this plan, other aspects of the oil industry could be kept out of the ANWR. No roads, pipelines, or human communities would be built on the refuge.

OIL AND THE ECONOMY

According to popular opinion polls, most Alaskans agree that oil drilling should be allowed in the ANWR. They often cite the economy of Alaska as an important reason.

Oil companies would pay billions of dollars for the right to drill in the ANWR. They also would hire thousands of workers. Many of these workers would come from the Prudhoe Bay oil fields. Without oil wells in the ANWR, these workers would be forced to find other jobs and likely would leave the state.

The oil industry employs many workers in Prudhoe Bay and Valdez. But money from oil helps people throughout the state. What major industries help the economy in your state? Would you want to help keep these industries in business?

PUBLIC PROTESTS

People disagree on many issues. But not all issues move people to stage rallies and protests. In recent years, people have rallied for and against the idea of drilling for oil in the ANWR. The ANWR issue has also been a part of many U.S. political campaigns, including the campaigns for president in 2008. So long as this oil remains untapped, the controversy is likely to continue.

Protestors in front of the U.S. Capitol in Washington, D.C. Despite the argument for drilling in the ANWR, many people are not convinced, and the debate continues nationwide.

Native Alaskans are shown here with a catch of salmon.

DRILLING IN ANWR:
THE CASE AGAINST

> "It is unacceptable that a nation is allowed to be destroyed for oil."
>
> *Luci Beach, executive director of the Gwich'in Steering committee, representing a group of native Alaskans.*

For thousands of years, the Arctic coast of Alaska has been home to the Inupiat and Gwich'in peoples. Some live in small villages, while others move from place to place in the region. These people survive by hunting. They hunt whales, caribou, fish, musk oxen, and many other Arctic animals.

Many Native Americans oppose drilling for oil in the **ANWR**. They believe that the oil industry would harm their way of life. They also fear accidents. A large oil spill in the Arctic would foul the water and kill a huge number animals. The damage would last for many years.

Organizations that are concerned about the environment also oppose ANWR drilling. They **cite** the natural beauty of the region and the risks of drilling there. Many U.S. government leaders, including President Barack Obama, have also expressed concerns.

Like those in favor of drilling in the ANWR, those opposed cite evidence in support of their ideas. Often the two sides cite the same scientific evidence, but analyze it in different ways. Scientists disagree about this evidence, too.

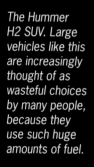

Two REVA G-Wiz electric cars, parked at charging bays in London, UK. Battery-operated electric vehicles like these are becoming more widely accepted as a good opti for moving away from oi

The Hummer H2 SUV. Large vehicles like this are increasingly thought of as wasteful choices by many people, because they use such huge amounts of fuel.

Making choices

Look again at the bar graph on page 30. It shows that the people of the United States continue to use more and more oil, yet the country's supply of oil is decreasing.

How can this problem be solved? Many people say that the answer is to **conserve** oil. To conserve something is to use it wisely, not wastefully. For an example, compare the automobiles shown here. The cars on the top are smaller and less powerful. However, in comparison they can travel much more efficiently than the larger car. Driving fuel-efficient or electric cars helps conserve resources like oil.

WORD STORE   **conserve** to use something sparingly

Where does electricity come from? In many cases, it comes from the burning of coal. Like oil, coal is a **fossil fuel** and is nonrenewable. Coal also causes many environmental problems, both when it is mined and when it is used.

Conservation groups encourage people to conserve electricity as well as gasoline. They also encourage alternatives to coal, especially from renewable resources. These alternative sources include wind power and solar power (power from the Sun). Another alternative is **geothermal energy**, which is the energy from Earth's hot interior.

What happens when it's gone?

Many organizations support conserving both energy resources and wildlife. These organizations include the League of Conservation Voters, the American Wildlife Federation, and the Sierra Club.

These organizations and many others argue that new Arctic oil would not lower the price of gasoline. But if we conserved gasoline, the demand for it would drop. Its price would drop as well.

Conservation groups also point out that the world's supply of oil is limited. If drilling is allowed in the ANWR, it would supply oil for a relatively short period of time. What happens next? What happens when all of Earth's oil runs out?

As nearly everyone agrees, we need to find a substitute for gasoline. As we have seen, many cars run on batteries or a combination of batteries and gasoline. Many people argue that we should invest more money in improving these kinds of cars, and that people should be encouraged to buy them.

"The controversy over the Arctic National Wildlife Refuge is a side issue."

said Kenneth Deffeyes, a geology professor at Princetown University.

"The problem we need to face is the impending world oil shortage."

The Exxon Valdez, two days after striking the reef that caused the disastrous spill. Though the ship did not spill all of its oil, the amount spilled would have filled about 125 olympic-sized swimming pools.

Disaster

When oil is mined and transported, workers take great care to keep it from spilling. Companies also must follow laws and policies that protect the environment. Nevertheless, as we have seen, oil spills have happened in the past. No one can guarantee that they will not happen again in the future. Concern over oil spills is another reason why many people oppose drilling in the ANWR.

The worst oil spill in the history of the United States occurred on March 24, 1989. An oil tanker named the *Exxon Valdez* ran aground off the southern coast of Alaska. It spilled about 40 million liters (11 million gallons) of oil into the water. The oil spread across the ocean and washed onto the shore. It killed hundreds of thousands of birds and other animals in the region.

Crude oil mixes poorly with water, but it can spread quickly on the water's surface. It also is very sticky. A bird or fish that is covered in oil cannot clean the oil off its body. It will die very quickly.

Tanker accidents in other parts of the world have spilled much more oil than the *Exxon Valdez* spilled. But the southern coast of Alaska is a far-off region that is difficult to reach. Cleanup crews took a long time to reach the oil spill, and the delay made the damage worse.

Today, scientists continue to find evidence of damage from the *Exxon Valdez*. The spilled oil left poisonous chemicals along the shoreline. The poisons were taken up by plants, then passed to animals that eat the plants. Scientists believe that sea otters, ducks, and salmon are dying at increased rates because of the poisons in their food chain.

As supporters of drilling argue, many new safety precautions are helping to prevent oil spills. Nevertheless, many people argue that the damage can be too great and is not worth the risk.

If oil spilled in the ANWR, it likely would come from an oil well or a small pipeline. Yet even a small oil spill would be difficult, if not impossible, to clean up properly. The region could suffer huge, long-lasting damage.

This oil-covered bird was found about a week after the spill, 56 km (35 mi.) from the accident.

The debate continues

All people agree that an oil spill in the ANWR would be a terrible event. But even if no oil were spilled, how would drilling in the ANWR affect people and wildlife there? Those in favor of drilling in the ANWR claim that it could be done with very little harm, if any, to the environment. But opponents claim otherwise.

Drilling for oil in the Arctic involves searching the waters with air guns, building **exploratory rigs** and **oil platforms**, and building roads and pipelines. Thousands of people must do this work. Would all of this activity harm the wildlife of the ANWR, even if it were kept to the smallest amount of land possible?

A polar bear and her cubs seen near Barrow, Alaska. Would polar bears suffer if oil wells were drilled near their home? Opponents of drilling claim the risk is too great.

Many small towns and villages lie on the Arctic coast, but only one is in the ANWR. This is the village of Kaktovik.

In 2006 the mayor of Kaktovik called one of the oil companies in the region "a hostile and dangerous force." The mayor argued that the company's drilling in the Arctic was harming bowhead whales. The villagers hunt these whales.

However, the people of Kaktovik are not against the idea of drilling for oil in the ANWR. They would support drilling if they were convinced it would be done properly and safely.

The people of Kaktovik depend on the Arctic Ocean. If oil is to be drilled there, they want their opinions heard.

Opponents of drilling say yes, absolutely. For evidence they cite the changes to Prudhoe Bay. The land and coast of Prudhoe Bay once looked much like the ANWR looks today. The photo on page 20 shows what Prudhoe Bay looks like today.

Where would it stop?

Many opponents of drilling believe the issue is much larger than one wilderness area in Alaska. In the past, oil companies and some political leaders have proposed drilling in other wilderness areas. If drilling is allowed in the ANWR, would places in the United States such as Yellowstone National Park and the Grand Canyon be next?

As the human population keeps expanding and growing, there are fewer and fewer places for wildlife to live and grow. Parks, wilderness areas, and nature reserves were established to preserve wildlife and to keep human development in check.

THE HIDDEN COST OF
OIL

Oil must be searched for and found. It must be taken out of the ground, then shipped and **refined**. All of these activities cost money, and all help contribute to the price of oil that people pay.

Yet oil has hidden costs for us, too. We do not pay these costs when we fill up the tanks of our cars. Instead we pay these costs in other ways.

Oil causes many kinds of pollution. When gasoline is burned, it releases compounds of nitrogen and sulfur into the air. This can lead to **smog**, an ugly form of air pollution. Oil also can pollute the water, as oil spills show.

Another kind of pollution from oil is more difficult to observe and study, and it is perhaps the most damaging. Look at the photo on this page. One hundred years ago, much of the Arctic Ocean was covered in ice all year long. Today, more Arctic ice melts during the summer than ever before.

Warmer temperatures are being observed not only at the poles, but also all across Earth. Scientists **cite** strong evidence that the use of oil, coal, and other **fossil fuels** is the cause.

This iceberg was once part of a glacier in Greenland. Now it has broken off of the glacier and water streams off of it as it melts.

Lead

In the 1920s oil companies began adding lead to gasoline. A compound made with lead helped engines run better. Unfortunately, lead is poisonou even in very small amounts. Most people did not know this at the time.

As the use of gasoline continued, lead built up in the environment. Doctor and scientists began observing the dangers of lead, especially in young children. Lead can cause brain damage and other disorders.

Finally, in the 1970s the United States banned lead in gasoline and other products. Today, only a few countries allow the use of lead. Yet while the problem of leaded gasoline has mostly been solved, other problems remain.

Smog

As we have seen, oil is made mostly of the elements carbon and hydrogen But it also contains small amounts of other elements, including nitrogen and sulfur. When a car's engine burns gasoline, these elements join with oxygen and become gases. The gases are released into the air with the car's exhaust. On warm, sunny days, the gases can form smog.

Smog can be seen here, hanging over Los Angeles, Califonia.

WORD STORE   petroleum another word for oil

Kurt Vonnegut was a famous U.S. writer of science fiction. In 2006, he offered words of wisdom about oil. "We're crazy, going crazy, about petroleum," he said. "It's a drug."

Vonnegut's point was that Americans continue to use and demand oil, even as the drawbacks of oil keep mounting. Oil causes pollution, it is expensive, and most of it must be imported from other countries. The governments of some of these countries are not friendly to the United States, but Americans still buy their oil. We know there are reasons to stop using oil, so why can't we stop? Are we addicted?

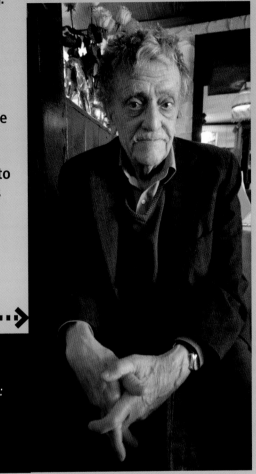

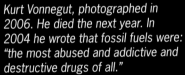

Kurt Vonnegut, photographed in 2006. He died the next year. In 2004 he wrote that fossil fuels were: "the most abused and addictive and destructive drugs of all."

Smog is a problem in many large cities. It can build up in the air and act like an ugly cloud. Severe smog can make the air harmful to breathe. To stop smog, many governments set strict standards for automobile exhaust. They often require cars to be inspected regularly.

Gasoline also can cause land and water pollution. This can happen when gasoline leaks out of holding tanks at service stations. Gasoline also leaks from the engines of cars or trucks. In 1996 a poison from gasoline leaked into the water supply of Santa Monica, California. The city was forced to shut down many of its wells.

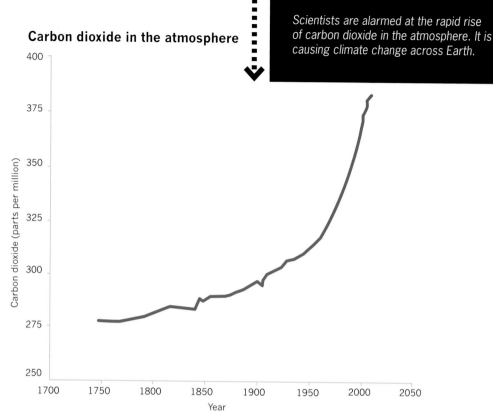

Carbon dioxide in the atmosphere

Scientists are alarmed at the rapid rise of carbon dioxide in the atmosphere. It is causing climate change across Earth.

Carbon dioxide (parts per million)

400

375

350

325

300

275

250

1700   1750   1800   1850   1900   1950   2000   2050

Year

A changing climate

For at least the past 50 years, scientists have been recording increasing temperatures all around the world. Glaciers have been melting, as has the ice near both the North Pole and South Pole. Weather stations in many places report record-high temperatures during summer and winter.

The rise in Earth's average temperature is often called global warming. However, a better name for the problem is global climate change. Rising temperatures are causing all sorts of other changes to Earth's climate. Some places may become rainier, and others may become drier. Hurricane and other severe storms are likely to become more common, too.

What is causing global climate change? A few scientists think it is part of a natural cycle of Earth's weather. But most scientists point to a different cause. They cite the increasing use of fossil fuels, including oil.

When oil and fossil fuels are burned, they release a gas called **carbon dioxide**. Carbon dioxide acts to trap heat and raise the air temperature. As the above graph shows, the levels of carbon dioxide in Earth's atmosphere have risen higher for the past 50 years. This corresponds to people's increasing use of fossil fuels.

WORD STORE   **carbon dioxide** byproduct of burning fossil fuels

Evidence shows that temperatures in the Arctic are rising twice as fast as other places on Earth. Scientists predict that by the year 2100, the ocean could be free of all ice during the summer.

Many critics, with some sadness, point out a relationship between global warming and Arctic oil. People's use of oil has caused Earth's temperatures to rise, which in turn has caused Arctic ice to melt. The melting ice will make it easier to drill for more oil in the Arctic, which will make the problem even worse.

Record-high temperatures and melting glaciers have been reported across all of Alaska, as well as places around the world. Scientists point to fossil fuels as the cause.

WORTH THE RISK?

Should we develop new oil fields in the Arctic, especially if they are part of a nature reserve? Many people have firm and fixed answers to this question. Others are not as certain. Many people are looking to find a compromise.

People on both sides of the issue **cite** the opinions of scientists and scientific evidence. As we have seen, scientists can explain how oil in the Arctic could be mined and shipped. They also can identify benefits and drawbacks to using oil, as well as the risks that oil poses to the environment.

However, scientists do not decide questions of public policy, such as whether or not to drill in the **ANWR**. In the United States, these questions are decided by the people and their leaders.

Now that you are at the end of this book, what is your opinion? Do you think that drilling for oil in the ANWR is worth the risk? Should we stop drilling for new oil and begin **conserving** the oil supplies we have? Or are you looking for a compromise that would partly satisfy everyone?

Your opinion matters! Decisions about oil are being made today, and they will affect your life in the future.

TIMELINE OF ARCTIC OIL EXPLORATION

1956 The U.S. government established the Interstate Highway System, a set of freeways that now span the country.

1960 A nature reserve, now called the Arctic National Wildlife Refuge (ANWR), was established in northeast Alaska.

1962 Oil discovered in northern Siberia, a province of Russia.

1968 Oil discovered in Prudhoe Bay, Alaska.

1977 Construction completed on the Trans-Alaska Pipeline System.

1980 Researchers estimated that the Arctic coast of ANWR holds up to 17 billion barrels of oil.

1989 Tanker *Exxon Valdez* ran aground on Alaska's southern coast, spilling nearly 40 million liters (11 million gallons) of oil.

1996 U.S. President Bill Clinton vetoed a bill to open ANWR to oil drilling.

1998 Prudhoe Bay oil production peaked at 2 million barrels per day.

2005 Democrats blocked an attempt by Senator Ted Stevens, Republican of Alaska, to open ANWR for oil drilling.

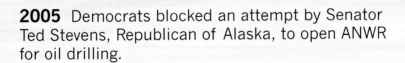

2008 Faced with rising gasoline prices, Americans began to favor increased oil drilling, including in ANWR.

GLOSSARY

Alaska Pipeline (also called Trans-Alaska Pipeline System) a long pipeline system that carries oil from north to south across Alaska

Arctic National Wildlife Refuge (ANWR) a region of northeast Alaska set aside for wildlife, and a site of oil reserves along its coast

carbon dioxide byproduct of burning fossil fuels, and a likely cause of global climate change

cite to refer to something

conserve to use something sparingly, saving its supply for the future

crude oil oil as it exists underground or is mined at oil rigs; unrefined oil

directional drilling drilling an oil well at an angle from an oil rig into the ocean floor

exploratory rig small oil rig built to search for oil deposits

fossil fuel a type of fuel, such as coal, oil, or natural gas, that forms from the remains of ancient plants and animals

geologist scientist that studies Earth's surface and interior

geothermal energy energy from Earth's hot interior

hydrocarbon compound, such as a fossil fuel, made of carbon and hydrogen only

hydrogen fuel cell device similar to a battery that runs on hydrogen and produces electricity

icebreaker a ship that can break ice apart to move across ice-covered waters

mammal warm-blooded animal that makes milk for its young. Ocean mammals include whales and dolphins.

natural gas a fossil fuel, made of methane, that often forms above oil deposits

oil platform a large oil rig built to mine oil, typically with many wells

oil rig an artificial island built for mining oil from beneath the ocean floor

petroleum another word for oil

refine a process of removing impurities by separating a substance into compounds

smog a form of air pollution caused by burning coal or oil

FIND OUT MORE

BOOKS

Horn, Geoffrey M. *Cool Careers: Oil Rig Roughneck*. Pleasantville, NY: Gareth Stevens, 2008.

Mercer, Ian. *Oils and the Environment*. Mankato, MN: Stargazer, 2005.

Smil, Vaclav. *Oil: A Beginner's Guide*. Oxford, Eng.: Oneworld, 2008.

Taylor, Barbara. *Arctic and Antarctic*. New York: Dorling Kindersley, 2000.

WEBSITES

Alyeska Pipeline
www.alyeska-pipe.com
Learn about the Alaska Pipeline from the company that built and operates it.

EIA Energy Kids
http://tonto.eia.doe.gov/kids/
This website from the U.S. Energy Information Administration is all about energy.

NASA Quest: Arctic Exploration Online
http://quest.arc.nasa.gov/arctic/
Discover the Arctic Ocean with the National Aeronautics and Space Administration (NASA), the agency of the U.S. government that explores space.

Arctic National Wildlife Refuge
http://arctic.fws.gov
Read more about the Arctic National Wildlife Refuge and the animals that live there.

Kaktovik, Alaska
www.kaktovik.com
Read about the village of Kaktovik, Alaska, which is in the Arctic
National Wildlife Refuge, and learn about its residents' opinions of
oil exploration in the Arctic.

TOPICS TO LEARN MORE ABOUT

- **Environmental concerns**
  Do further research on the Arctic environment, and the specific
  concerns people have about oil drilling in that environment.
  What kinds of ecosystems are present in the Arctic? What
  makes them unique? How much would they be changed or
  damaged due to activities such as drilling and construction?

- **Moving beyond oil**
  We know that oil is a disappearing resource, but can we survive
  without it? Research alternative and renewable energy sources,
  such as hydro, wind, nuclear, and solar power. What are the
  pros and cons of each option? Are there other possible energy
  sources that are still being developed? If the world ran out of oil
  today, could humanity survive?

INDEX

j 622 HARTMAN
Hartman, Eve.
Searching for Arctic oil

j 622 HARTMAN
Hartman, Eve.
Searching for Arctic oil

GAYLORD